A LIGHT WORKER

AND TRUCKERS, AND OTHER POEMS

Clarke

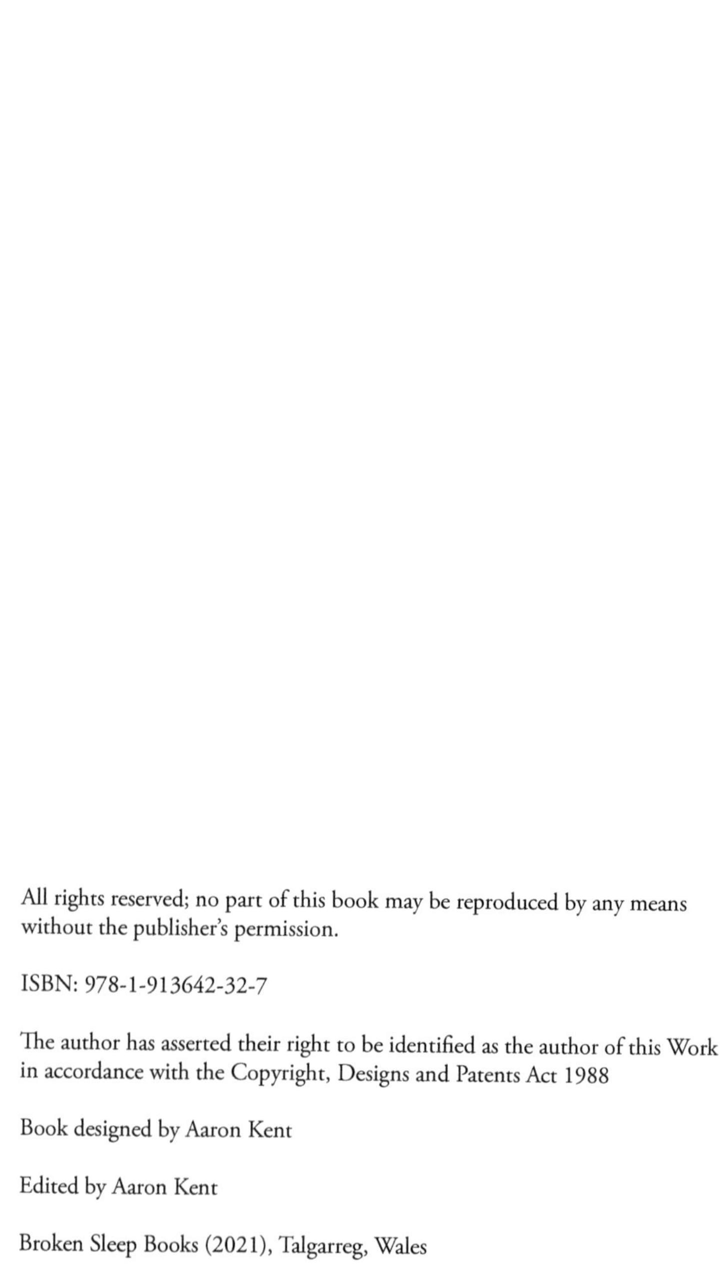

ISBN: 978-1-913642-32-7

Book designed by Aaron Kent

Edited by Aaron Kent

Broken Sleep Books (2021), Talgarreg, Wales

Contents

A Light Worker

Lucy Harvest Clarke

A Light Worker

I Am Not Free

When we visit it's always to the lightness
Eyes half closed
The secret visitors
I don't trust colours nor
Shadows any more
I can't feel in my centre
Like the sea
As in nothing like
The light on the sea
In my middle
My small duty
To the patient birds
That we share be crawing
The warning
"One more. One more"
How many springs may we witness here?
Windows ajar

The first thing I know is an absence
Somehow like addition of rain
The silence under a plummet
That moves above by time
How long can anyone stand it?
Existing with a truth beset

Where is freedom anyway
Some diamond on the shore
Witness to each earthly theft

May the simple pools stay with you
Your eyes by any body of water
Mirroring the wide mouth of dusk

When we return to our work
We see our work is about webs
Webs are but made up and cosmos
Mitts for outgrowing the world

To therefore hold the self
Pent up to the night
The interior network
Holds no boat with time

In the beginning there is
ABC
A sea of bees
A screaming theme

Let me sleep like I don’t know I’m here

The Wreck of Calendars

Now that my heart is outside myself
As I lent breath my white brick
As the sky cannot ceiling
Since harbouring such clutch

As if each day a bubble
Soot marbles for eyes
Each morning mumbles
Fawning and up the creek again

Just now in some haze
The bliss of the closed world
The cold dead world

Stay lidded
Stay closer

Each morning is closing
Finishing on ender-upper

Since money sieves moments
Objects lofted

Art plays grandeur
The splendour of the lean
And the wreck of calendars

I'd dozen another
Except my heart lands
Always rinsing away

Time splintered in cleaning
Then the fall in
Atomically moved on
I clamber on dust

The third hand is the fastest

Stomp
Stomp
Loss

It's in your basement
Each simple breakage
In your sleeping bag
Sweet as the present
Cramped like ribs up
Need to space places
Hold the good notes
Stuck of time
Going to stake me
What are you saying?
You wouldn't touch which

Spiral things/ Spinning

Cargo

the voice of the car

cannot

I called

but the only place is

this place

in the car

as I can

just but

not so much as in

but of

(the car)

I hope

to make

moving

an act

what is to be

all alone with that

what is to be

done with that

lo what

can we do

but here

and there

consecutively

but it's

not just that though

is it

it's this what

of mine

it's about

which was

a thing

I'm driving round

to see

if I can do

and I do

whole heartedly

do

it fills up in me

but here

I'd like to see

the time

of the car thing

mirrored

I said please

I must have

but I said it

in an old fashioned way

I don't know what

the old fashioned way

is but

that is the way

I make myself

forget

how difficult you have been

for looking at

even us we

know it's

a different way

this time

realising as it did

then

and will be

for all

times

that I bereft

and vote

this as one

if asked

which I can’t

tell on

if theres a want to

only you can

mirror your

only elements

which are the way

to only I

up in my way

this way place

I’ve become

I’ve re-done it

darling

I've sent it I have

and have

always done so

for as I now on

in know

this old song

to your meadow

stays on the right

the unnamed

old way

to get to

you in

some kind

of fine

format I swear

when a face talks

I predict

everything

this way if

It's not

the skin

it’s the eyes

if it’s not the

so on

It’s not

here enough

so

Be3a

Cigarette factory
6 and you're home
in this coat
you feel
isotropic - from
the factory
on your bicycle
through the violent
universe carving
epicycles - you know
all gravity must go
on alone
you can feed the
endless now inside you
you can feel some
warmth behind snake
up on you in a
sense war

Dry lagoon
you decide it on
familiar words
still her salt
civil like tears
never sunned
in an orange dress
you were not
to sweat in
labour though
water you say
very good at escaping
where it will
and with it
your love ferocious
feeding daily
a world water
waged memory
the glass lagoon

Ring dance
The so-called
secret god
ring maned
you ring dance
a secret black
name for good
to make the tip off
an inland see
you cannot reach
the head land
you feel you could
use better
a beach slap
than a trace
lace foam
dear black dust
you left us

Soft closing
you are born
a billion seconds ago
a light worker
october ghost
certainly you soon
outgrow with lake
the single horizon
double tailed
you summer school
breaking free
nor the piano
or the metal windows
but out to the frozen
a mixed drink
soft closing
on a black dusk

Square sun
you don't
come heavy
to the square
but the sway
of your lungs
glint no
glint glint
no glint
see them make
a blindness lit
A sense you are
a nape
an example
but so up trenched
in your only life
your arms
automatic make
swimming motions

Tulsi
where is your duty
where is your patient
in wonder at
any dedication
you think of animals
an answer to the land
uninterpreted
you bring science
some people fire visions
others salt meat
you take plant
you suffer plaited
dislodged squat
here by fells
a hungry animal
will attack
though it is
love you make

Tara

It's an open elevator up to the loft
An open cage
Our mothers in jewels

Tara your life was America to me
Mickey ears Tara
Bubble gum roll

New York Tara and the new me was you
You had what I wanted
Princess Tara

The sequins shiver now
Satin rose
And you should not ever have known

In Formentera I slapped a Spanish women
Her face in my face
She got too close

But you never did that
Did you Tara
Now envy my own hand to hold

Eyes out on the open street
In 1996 the grit pores in to us
We triangle styles below your home

Were you told our mothers shared
The sidewalk was a different place then - Tara
With hope for a different place

She was held up by her hair
Trying to explain pain to a daughter who has
A daughter but she laughs

Slapping the ocean in a long lost tiara
She smacks the deadest cat
Tara - my sorry oysters

Forgive me I should've known you better
My stars tipped with guilt
As we write all luck sickens me

I wish to hold off your death
On Sunset Park
Spilling out his secrets

Spooling out the liberty
That left your life
From a woman's neck

I wear your all is not lost t-shirt
But I don't mark your death - Tara
I can't mark your death.

Blue door/ Blood donor

Some swallows are lonesome
    they solemn the skies
We look up the same way each time
Who part sad that seek for here
    a currency to echo

To deal with the instrumental version of life
My old me is alive in the hold
    got space as is fine
    like a doctor
    ripped and half rippled with kind
Ingests all her digits inside and that lockets

This air in the strong hold of glory
Under water makes deadly bright
Taking daily honestly
    would corrupt any double
    than either these two minds

And yes for the surge
        of my vein on the verge
Off the shoulder side
        near to near blind

A fall in is as good as a reach
        as the line of day sight
        turns white with common law

Scandalous the ahead of back electrics
All orange or gone by lamp light
It is those whitest of mountains
        with independent eyes

My finest decisions cellular
Skills and renditions liberally circular
        rotating slow
        that's how we get ago

Allow these almond birds to drive freely
        they are land locked completely
Bound to the cupping skies

The frequency of diffusal
        a disguised about face
Any church chime can set it wandering

Any hallway you come to
For the rest of your days
        a fixed carpet
        could truth a displace

We like trapdoors
We don't explain why

I'll get a night in to surrendering a day
I'm in a large hall
        we don't exist, we claim
Ascend out up and away as bright
        I'm a stair thrower you say

        corrosive lust attends
And it all might love with the night
        with no end

Some kinds of union are like this they fear
If you chance to find yourself
        close by his open window
        touch the window
Until everything mirrors

If you close your eyes with lasting enough
You can be anywhere in your life
            as a singular hum
            hones your ear

Nocturnal birds are so cunning
            rise before the canopy comes
And so alone
That's a school
We pass it

The parts are in half
Either side of a chimney stack
            hanging wild in the corners
Abandoned wardrobes

My borders solely mine
            and reclining

Storms relive their ownership
            in 12 year cycles
When comes the time
            it's home versus home
And there is no need to forgive

Cadmium and lightning strikes
Moon bowl in a blue light
            dust every 8th tune

The same elbow on the throat
Holds the head up that hopes
            and have you
Held it up to the morning

That sunlight inky upon us
Why I really get to feel
            my way to the bus

Truckers

"When she said at first I did not quick

Breathe in and know the ocean
Breathe out and see the water

Actually I fathomed and writhed
Actually I swept up
The cage

Water is
And becoming of these

When all comes over
All are gone
Returns then a sun"

Truckers. In Glory

Free lights, coasting darkness

A high way, a free way

On a coast road. On any road

On that one way, under metal

In metallic armour

Love is blind, nothing awaited

Nothing owed, but if it tasted

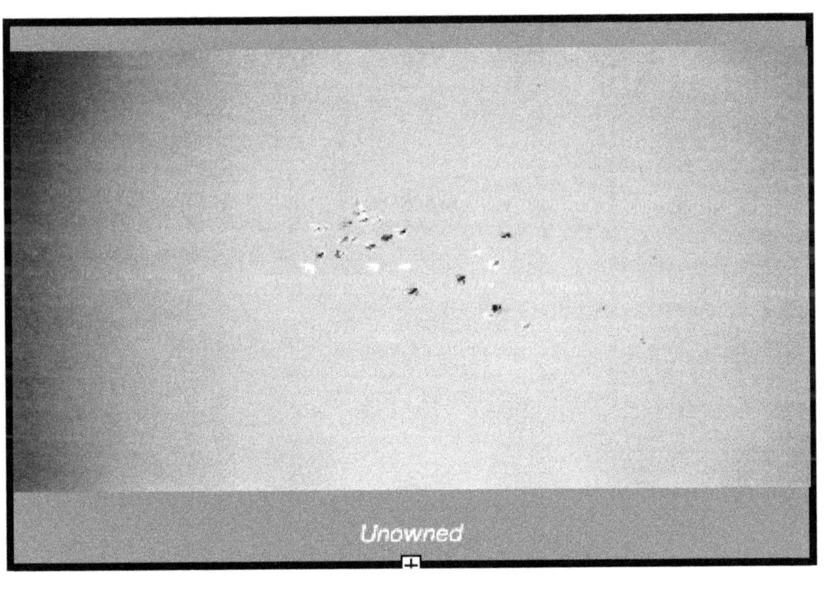
Unowned

Honour your partner

truckers
undertakers
livers of lives
men as sons

the harbour
the hawks
a cry for help
run round the world

actually billions?
yes billions of years
throughout
and about
your sodden forehead
on a bunch of sea

break it up
docey high
docey low
one more round
and balance it home

the garden gate
in dear respoe
a certain calm cloth
been down
the done and dust
the owl round eggs
love exactly
and non exactly
let the rain wash up

you make yourself
sit through
these times

of longing
left open
like a want
of which we are not
but the pink
sky lamp
still comes right up

like a bloody echo
bare witness do we
held but for the eye
blink and you
night my dream
wink and we get tight

crush is at home
every tomb is whistling
bouyant borderlines

when all is spilt over
all's left is the body
which you cannot deny
the cave zone
the rave place

stooped with a jar
under pines

your face can be
receiving the world

my body is
receiving the world

my body chooses
to meet the world

O Comely O Domestic

Down in the deep of the land cape
O comely O domestic

Down at the depth met zero
Keep on just wept horizon
My heart would not stop what's left

Deeper yet in serried conception
The thin in-let cosmic verse
Unpicked and strewn
What I could do not to you

And the water moon producing

Lower to the depths of certainty
Lowered reaching under so much to do
Stacked up in mood gravities
Yo peel the morn yo don't my turn
And please say sorrel

Here comes the lowly rattle
Read shake your heart treads

Patterns of the unlit
Where you are you so careful

Fires at the border crossing

Peachy here comes the base train
Follow the rooky down

Deep down the broken trail
My love so crassly done

The chicken snaps like a wish
The valley with any old rumble

Your ruckus of a crave to
Tell the rising
Enter at the finger bones

Please someone charity the elbow
At the shoulder

A divine car full

matter is the coolest dead
the cry of the living world

too true heart for flatness
englobed in the rock light

a whole future is held in a hand

theses songs of the longing left
there for the hearts of the wanting

how the car's always full
or sealed by window frost

each dormant mouse upon mouse

beckoning from the locked house
I'm my own cat burglar

please can we do that thing where
you make yourself stare through

every third breath a commuter takes off

my one guess already given
and I'm the ghost of

Untitled (for Keira)

black smith

black john

you wild dog

soft defences

of portraits

hold outlines

they skate

pinching ovals

fled to the hot springs

held out for the desert

cut grasses

rolling stones

so come to it now

my sunning love

the self

a mere morsel

of impeccable

and awful

time travel

you rose water

up to those

the moment

froze when

all lit light

became in coloured

by nowness

of all the loves

your luckerless best

holds thumbs out

asking just

be warm winds

be courage enough

attest to

life's own breath

by the realness

the death

Other Poems

Grass

A history of corn a remembrance is but a long list of all I've lost or parts that are of the self lacking. That maudlin affair. A field a foray in to yesterday and yester year is all that that ever was - at the foot of the garden. A hanging bird. A hallucination of an eagle. Battling swords as twigs that break on contact remembering diluted present though answers to questions future remembers and all for the garden. The yield? The crop?

Is drift off in to the corn the long and fallowed field yellow the colour and purple though attaches it my high strong atache in wielded yearning my learning turning and wanting. Wanting and knowing like always knowing. The pigeon sounds the dove. The duck goes. There is a shooting there is a falling.

Walking down the path hawthorns in tyres hawthorns in heels and nettles dandelions cowslip and docs falling on to a bed of nettles that makes me urtica rich long after my many hormonal axis shift my balance the nettles must come out and they swell my fingers and push my child out. My skin burns from the spring sun with blisters that are untimely children whilst the one who made it through itches and I leave.

The pastures are burdened by lawns. The neighbours work the finest land and the lambs are born under lamps laying on straw they are fed and kept alive. The pastures are interjected by a path a free way a run way a mown tenderness. The hawthorns churned by the mower need to be collected in fragments.

Apples are mushed and wasp invaded collected by the mower. The path entrance a place of border a lawn through a pasture. Solar shone the solar over plastic is oilless in a cold night house the blankets and the lightning strike the lights collapse and whirr.

When I run it is in great disbelief only the loneliness knows how to hurt me. I cried to the oak at the end gnarly and nobly treed I still need to feed and cry in to a self made there on a tree shelf perches as elf and sat for many hours till temper tones and failure returns as just a commitment as is to have grass. All lowered and shortened and unnoticed but for the diaries and the collected lists and the peering from the orchard.

"What my heart first waking whispered the world was"
- *Elizabeth Smart*

Salad

I once made a thing you know
but us we sure do addicts
I called it shove as were story
sort of like by anonymous
I used to sit here on my break
watch them eat their bits
gurgle and drink and gaggle
and when they looked up
I'd look back at my papers
I thought that love so silken
and I loved it like white snow
but we are a moving peoples
you know we got to move
make changes to stuff go on
one day it just clicked
and I started to get in cars
it was better than sitting
waiting for intentions
even if the illness weren't
but people are easy to read
you just look at their face
some are self happy with
others got the ghouls
others just floating wood
all manner of these out there
and I was just the compulsed
like I had a destination disease
oft times I had no pillow
or water rattling dry
but those were the days of days
the ones that turn in
now I'm a healthy mama
I put salad in my cigarettes
and a disco ball is just them stellas
spinning one way

and the floor the other
I can still hold in my stuff
at the seafront by the warm sea wall
I think of this as a whole glory
she looking good in socks
after the storms it were hardest
a lot of wet on the ground
that's when only the lonely
I remember it on the dash
I was knowing then the horizon
and none of the two parts were my fault
I didn't really exist till I got here
for the best they say
as being alone you are
a sole misdemeanour
and that's better than a conspiracy

Cards

It was august tomorrow and the cards had arrived. It all started in a town many towns from there and the roads hadn't been born. So far the roads had the twinkly light that mother and great mothers in silence were. It was awkward not sad just redundant to mention the azul of the sea or the times. She heralded the strings of a door in a triangle and we are here again bending one knee. Why will to arrive at this momento whom all days must pass and hang low. It was summer yet and it is always here and none here think to escape. Still nightmares retain cold looks at night and are repeatedly over chosen.

What happened to the visuals of this was concrete. It crisped and cupped and he was never arriving, that cards in the post made elation. And just the thought of cards in the post kept the bed in the house and the house on the earth, in the day at most, inferring life. Town as no fixed work on horizon having effect of continual work. Work the word is underused and is creeping on to them like cossacks. Spectaculars gently cascade where the background can be like muted graphite. Such strings are created course with beadiness, fabricada like lake-ocean.

To feel gravel and to feel such gold gravel, these luxuries where time stood still. The mind is the central glass. It is thin and deluxe like it wants to. We are already laying a bare floor but stretched out we are already a floor. She read that this and that is perfect and of space knows neither, how cranky! Under dorsal of cards a courtyard pastime we fickle and move and distract. Being back and in on the shadow map was easy in the tempraduro reale. It cannot hold such seas to such eras such ears and inquisitive glance. Just a button though just a popper romp. To pop and restrain in this dive.

You cannot co-ordinate nor talk your way down and out but it will arrive. You are here and of course you want that. If you'd had something silverlined you'd refrigerate. They progressed to disregard such halter kilter. It is forward to hold a buckle in a fist but when you cannot clench how will you keep?

December

December you have covered it all and cancelled the rest.

December I can see - when I exhale - you erase.

December white triangle rinsed on pink horizon.

December a type of peak.

You exist but you were also made, isn't that right December.

Something came out of the sky, it was black and cold, and we named it December.

With your white shadow you remain ostensibly futile.

But it was December that knocked on your grandmother's door.

December it is land now covered in chalk.

The birds of December hang from branches, still warm.

December settles on gravel as an interface and we simply cannot ignore you.

December I think you illuminate contrast.

With your contrasting sides December, I sense blood.

December put the year down the hole.

Despite an effort given December can never be tabloid.

Flat December like two hundred and twenty two.

For this cavernous back wall I thank you December.

You may be best all up and heathen, but you're also on the golf course, aren't you December.

December is the posthumous advert for life.

You are so upright December - not a bit satanic.

December I like that plain bread.

December holds refuge - a smoky one.

December holds a gang of birds in limbo.

We tried to spice you December but you didn't like it really.

So December in your encumbrance.

Hatted and boxed you must be like December.

Just December on a foot numb.

December look at your repeating poem.

With your worth and your tension you can encapsulate it December.

December trying calm disruption whispered 'winter' but this too was a fractured visage.

December when no letters affected you.

December you made an exit it seems.

December austere loving horses only.

I'm hoping to progress beyond you December.

December Mountains are still not made of bricks.
But, here we are, December again.

Between us we probably know best December.

December I always have you under the stairs.

December the cold creeper, you mongrel - you have proved yourself rigid all right!

In the courtyard the walls are drying now, trying to picture December.

I did my best not to own you December but you made it so very easy.

December your sugary crisp is stuck in my spine.

I think you were once in love, weren't you, December.

It's like you decided December.

December rolled up to the knee, allowing for a dip.

The wind is December - a jostle and a wrestle - so marvellously tender.

Tender December, blindfolded throwing butter knives.

December I beg you give me back my letters.

Oh dear December, what is it you want from me?

Your dark dark night December, your dark dark night.

December - black solstice black dog.

Please I need December to leave me.

You and your screaming trees December covering the skeleton.

The lead in a boot December.

December like a crooked gate.

Climb over it but you just get to – December.

December a bit wanton like a promise or a risk.

But do you end it, December?

December – the star that cut the left index.

So December curt and controlling.

In earnest December at each man equally.

With your way of sticking to the centre December.
And when he came it was December and morning.

All across the panels in a milky courtyard they couldn't quite put their finger on December.

Just the same as everything.

In this way you have to be December.

I remember the white walls.

Can't you cuddle up any other time.

December you have no opposite any more and no allies to speak of.

December you gave her real blue lashes.

I don't feel that caustic word December - I live for you now.
People know you are cleanish December.

Something in the glass made an epigram, and they named it December.

December likes touching my reading books.

Just a touch December.

Acknowledgements

Be3a first published by if p then q as a series of postcards 2018, Manchester. https://ifpthenq.co.uk/odditiies/clarke-lucy-harvest-be3a/

Blue door/ Blood donor appeared in Paratext issue 7 2019 London https://www.paratext.co.uk/index-to-issue-7

The quote in Grass on page 54 is from The Assumptions of the Rogues & Rascals by Elizabeth Smart (1978) published by Jonathon Cape London

LAY OUT YOUR UNREST

www.ingramcontent.com/pod-product-compliance
Ingram Content Group UK Ltd.
Pitfield, Milton Keynes, MK11 3LW, UK
UKHW020416250726
13967UKWH00007B/2671

9 781913 642327